Let's Go to Korea!

대한민국

To Jiang Myung Gee, my fallen soldier on the DMZ. You made the ultimate sacrifice in protection of the free. – 상관 대리

Artist: Michael Blendermann
Editor: Geoff Smith
Graphics: Inscribe

Copyright © 2016 by Tommy Tong
ISBN: Hardback – 978-1-940827-24-7
ISBN: Ebook – 978-1-940827-25-4
ISBN: Kindle – 978-1-940827-26-1

All rights reserved. No part of this book may be reproduced or transmitted in any form or by any means, electronic or mechanical, without permission in writing from the copyright owner.

Long ago before countries had names or anyone could write, people drifted across Asia in search for new lands to feed their families and grow their tribes. At that time, most people in the world were hunters and farmers who got their food from the land.

As people began to reach the sea and settle along the coasts they learned to make boats so they could catch fish from the ocean. One very special place where people could hunt in the mountains, farm in the fields and fish in the sea was to become known as Korea which means *"the tall and beautiful land"*.

Korea sticks out into the ocean from the mainland and is called a *peninsula*. Peninsulas are what we call land that is surrounded by water on three sides.

The peninsula of Korea is a little smaller than California in the United States and even has the same weather, but it is on the other side of the world across the biggest ocean, The Pacific. The Pacific was named by the famous western explorer Magellan and means "peaceful sea". In Asia, the Pacific is not always so peaceful.

Powerful storms would often sweep fishermen out to sea never to be heard from again. Some of these fishermen landed safely on islands that no one knew about until thousands of years later since none of those cast-away fishermen could return back home against the strong ocean currents.

Even though the people liked to eat fish from the sea, most of them preferred to stay on land where it was safe. They harvested food of all kinds from the lush fields and mountains.

Soon, there were many people in Korea and they wanted a king to protect them, give them rules to follow and, keep the peace. The tribes in the north were the first ones to receive such a man and his name was Dangun. He is the first person the Koreans wrote about and is remembered every year with a national holiday.

Very little is known about the king since he lived over 4,000 years ago. Back then, writing was a group of simple pictures carved into wooden books. The pictures are called pictograms and some still remain in many written languages in Asia.

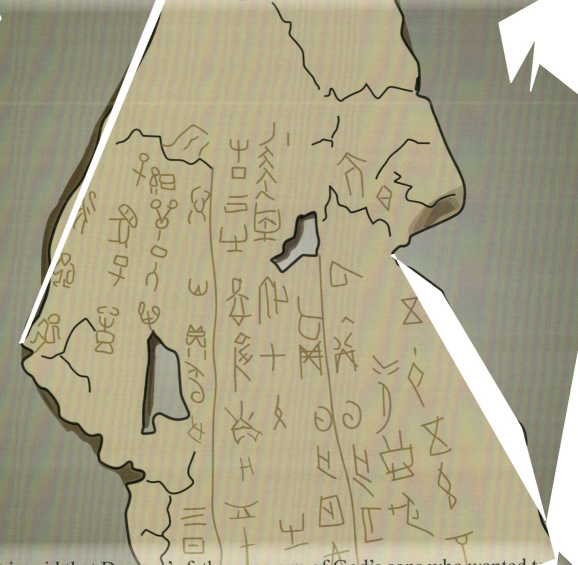

It is said that Dangun's father was one of God's sons who wanted to live on Earth. He came down from Heaven to Korea with some of his closest friends to build a city and rule the people of the nearby lands. When he returned to Heaven, he left his own son, Dangun, to lead the people and become their king.

Dangun sent Shaman around the land to teach people right from wrong and make rules for living together. It gave the people peace for thousands of years. Shaman were wise men who kept law and order almost like a judge does today. They also helped in special ways when people were in need.

The Koreans let other people come to their kingdom and learned new things from them. It made their cities grow bigger and faster. Most of these new people came from the area that is now called "China", bringing news and ideas from other parts of the world.

Soon the Korean people had some of the finest pottery in Asia, metal plows to use in their fields and farm animals to make life easier. It was a great time for the people and, their kingdom had grown to cover the northern half of the peninsula.

In the south, there was more land and fewer people. They were spread much further apart and didn't yet need a king since they had fewer newcomers and still lived in tribes or large families.

A tribe is like a small village where everyone knows each other and everyone is a friend or family member. If there are problems, the fathers or "elders" decide what to do.

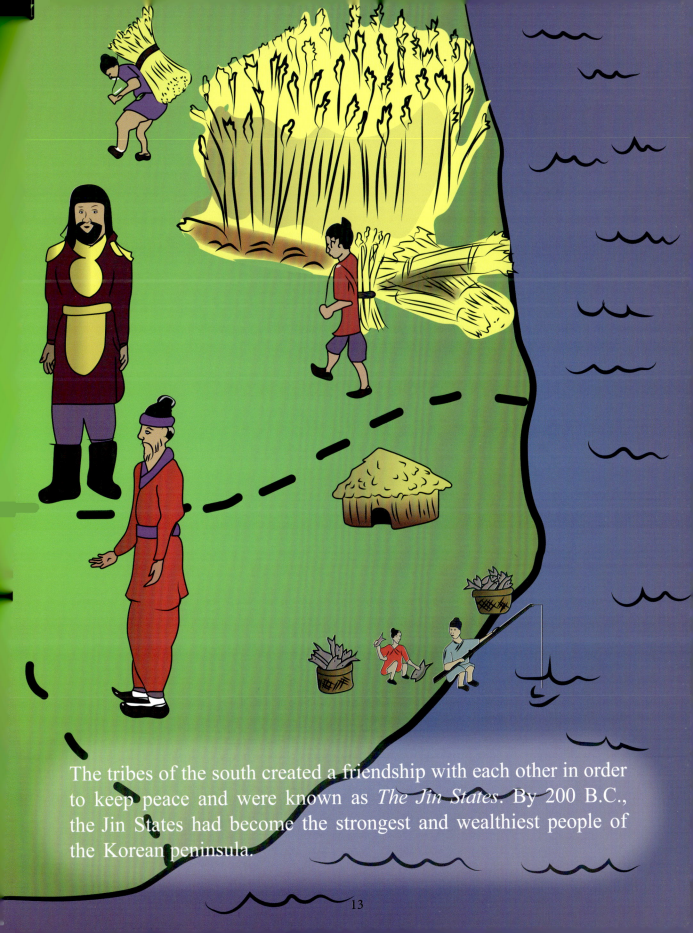

The tribes of the south created a friendship with each other in order to keep peace and were known as *The Jin States*. By 200 B.C., the Jin States had become the strongest and wealthiest people of the Korean peninsula.

Dangun's kingdom in the north got along with the tribes of South for hundreds of years and everyone kept busy growing their families and building their cities.

They enjoyed many of the inventions being created in China and even many of the teachings of wise men from all over the world. In return, the Korean people sent many gifts back to China's emperors.

One famous teacher from China was a man named Confucius. Confucius lived about 2,500 years ago and taught people to obey their parents and elders, take care of those younger than themselves and, be kind and courteous to everyone.

Confucius is one of the greatest teachers in history and his writings are studied by millions of people all over the world still today.

About the same time Confucius was teaching people in China, another great man was teaching people his wisdom in India. His name was Buddha and his words spread all over Asia, making their way to the people of Korea. Buddha's teachings would soon grow to become the largest religion in the world for 2,000 years and is still a very big one today.

Buddha taught that we are all eternal beings who only live on the planet for a short life-time before moving on. He said that we should not lie, cheat nor steal, and that we should never kill anything, not even a bug. All living things are precious and none of them should be harmed.

Buddha's teachings are still studied in most Asian countries today, though his practices have almost faded out in India where Buddha was from. But, people all over the world still recognize his face. Have you ever seen this man?

As the population of Korea grew, available land started to run out and people began to argue over who could use it.

The people of the south decided to build their own armies to protect them from the north and other tribes. Soon there were many armed kingdoms all over the land and some of them didn't get along very well.

For a thousand years the kingdoms fought among themselves trying to make their own lands bigger and more powerful than the others. They became afraid of one another and spent their time training soldiers and fighting battles instead of working in the fields. It was a very bad time for the people.

Great battles were fought all over the land and many great generals were created, but no kingdom was strong enough to unite them all. When one got too strong, the others would unite to prevent it from conquering everyone.

With the Koreans constantly fighting each other, the peninsula became vulnerable to attack by outsiders. During these troubled times, other countries would regularly attack the various kingdoms of Korea.

The Japanese attacked in the south, the Chinese in the west and in the north. Even the Mongolians tried to control the peninsula. But, like a big game board, no one could hold onto it for very long.

By now, the Koreans had some of the best soldiers in the world and were led by the wisest generals. They had better weapons and ships than the other countries too. Sometimes they won battles against enemies ten times their size with their special weapons and skills.

The Koreans also had a small but powerful navy. Their most famous ship was called a turtle ship because it had a spiked iron shell to protect it when fired upon or boarded. Armed with early missiles and fire cannons, the mighty ships defended Korea against all odds time and again.

Some people have called Koreans 'the Spartans of the east' because they were the best soldiers around and were always prepared to fight. Spartans were the fiercest warriors in all of Ancient Greece. They were trained to fight from a very early age and won many famous battles.

The Koreans developed a fighting style called Tae Kwon Do. It uses many kicks since the Koreans were farmers and had very strong legs from pulling their plows. Their hips also became very flexible from squatting down in their rice patties all day. Today, Tae Kwon Do is an Olympic sport and is very popular among children all over the world.

Finally, a powerful king from the north united the entire peninsula then defended it from outsiders. His name was King Taejo and he named his kingdom Goryeo.

From that day on, the world has called this important peninsula Goryeo but in the west people spell it Korea.

Though it was small, Korea was strong enough to convince the greatest conqueror of all times not to invade their land. Instead, Genghis Kahn accepted gifts and treasures and left Korea alone as he conquered most of the rest of Asia.

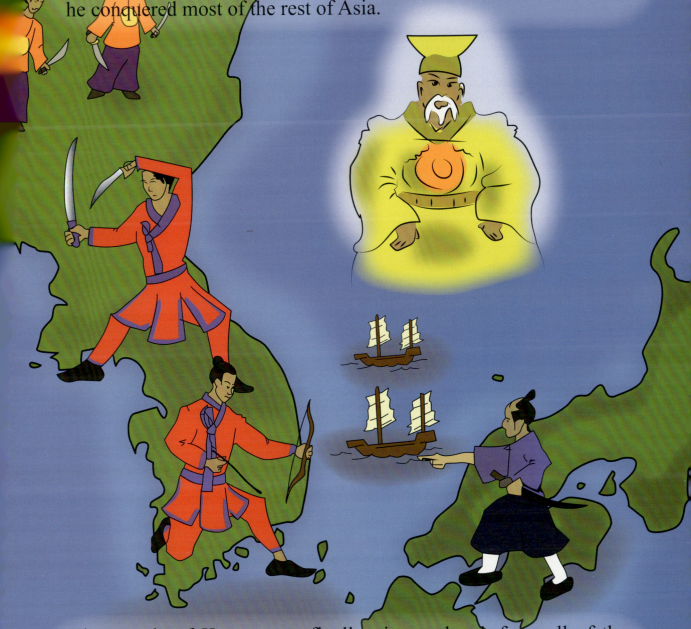

The people of Korea were finally given a break from all of the fighting and their peace lasted for hundreds of years while the Mongolians ruled over the Asian continent.

The Kingdom of Goryeo began to build temples and schools, create fine pottery and art, and learn new ways of thinking. Monks began to teach of Confucius and Buddha, children returned to school and soldiers left the army to go back to their farms.

The country grew rich in many ways and the people turned their minds towards peaceful inventions. They even invented one of the earliest printing machines and made thousands of wooden books.

The Koreans created stone carvings of Buddha in the mountains as well as many other monuments and temples. They also had more time for play as kids instead of doing their father's work while he was away in the army.

Koreans love "kimchi" and have many different kinds. Kimchi is made from cabbage, ginger, salt and other spices that are left to soak and ferment for weeks. Once it is ready, it is served as a side dish or even in soup.

Korea was attacked again and again throughout history and sometimes the enemy stayed for many, many years. But the Korean people always fought back and never gave up.

Today the peninsula is divided into two countries again. They argue and fight with each other from time to time and have to be kept apart by peacekeepers. But, they are still related to each other, speak the same language and want to be one country again someday.

South Korea is once again very rich and powerful. Its capital is Seoul and it is one of the largest cities in the world. They make many wonderful things and send them all over the world in huge ships. They have nice homes, expensive cars and many universities.

Unfortunately, North Korea has many problems. The people are poor and hungry because the country is not very well run. The leaders have not gotten along with other countries in the world and the people suffer greatly. North Korea spends most of its money on the military and have had the biggest one in the world for many years!

Most people think that Korea should be united into one country again, and both sides talk about it from time to time in a small village called Panmunjom. For many years it was the only place where people of the two countries would talk, and only for very important things.

Today people from the south can go into the north for work, but they must return home every night since it is very dangerous for them. Sometimes, people get taken prisoner in the north and don't return home for many years. Most westerners are not allowed to visit the north at all.

Someday the leaders of North Korea will decide to make peace instead of war and the people will be together again as one country. When that happens, a united Korea will become a very strong country indeed!

About the Author

Tong served inside the Korean demilitarized zone as a young UN officer in the year of Big Brother (1984). With many Korean soldiers in his platoon, Tommy soon learned the language, food, culture, customs, holidays and, merriment. At the time a decent suit would cost you $20 in town, popular western cassettes sold for $2 and a night out might cost you $10. Certainly affordable on soldier's pay. Alas, Korea's GNP has tripled since then and, though it is still worth the fare, a night out will cost you ten times as much now.

Tong's R&R program for his men included river rafting campouts a few miles off the front, beach exercises down south, armed ski trips to the east and cultural visits around the countryside. Similar to California in seasons and landscape, it is a fascinating land few people know much about. It is said that a king once threw a fit over people chewing on their wooden chopsticks so, he required metal chopsticks from that day forward. And let me tell you, they a smaller, thinner and a whole lot tougher to use. Don't try them at home!

Look for other amazing titles by Tommy Tong…

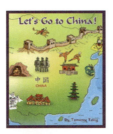 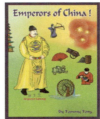 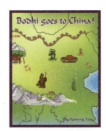

  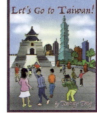